5-Minute Proofreading Practice

180 Quick & Motivating Activities Students Can Use to Practice Essential Proofreading Skills—Every Day of the School Year

Jill Safro

Edited by Mela Ottaiano
Cover design by Brian LaRossa
Cover art by Jim Paillot
Interior design by Holly Grundon
Interior illustrations by Mike Moran

ISBN-13: 978-0-545-16833-5
ISBN-10: 0-545-16833-3
Copyright © 2003, 2009 by Jill Safro
All rights reserved. Published by Scholastic Inc.
Printed in the U.S.A.

1 2 3 4 5 6 7 8 9 10   40   15 14 13 12 11 10 09

5-Minute Proofreading Practice

Contents

Introduction

Wat wuold happin ifnobody pfoofred nothing thay rote? This wood!

An extreme example? Certainly. But there's no denying that the skill of proofreading is one that should be mastered by everyone. Searching for and correcting our own mistakes are critical steps in any writing endeavor.

The proofreading habit is one that is best started early, when students are still learning language arts skills and gaining an appreciation for the wonders of the written word. The goal of this book is to kick-start what's sure to be a lifelong labor of love.

What's Inside This Book and Companion CD

Inside this book, you'll find 180 reproducible proofreading problems, covering essential skills such as spelling, capitalization, punctuation, usage, and more. They are specifically tailored to introduce kids to the power of proofreading, reinforce language arts skills, and elicit a few smiles, to boot. The companion CD features the same 180 proofreading problems you may use with a SMART Board™.

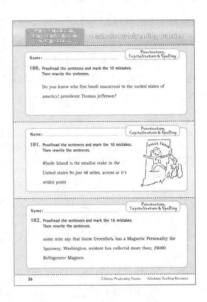

How to Use the Book

Whether students work on one problem or several at a time is entirely your decision. Simply reproduce the pages within, clip apart, and distribute activities to students in amounts that are suited to your daily schedule and curriculum needs. While intended as independent-learning exercises, you may also consider having student pairs work on problems (especially those with multiple errors). Try using these as day-starters, exit passes, or even quick quizzes.

Keep in mind that many of the problems require students to mark mistakes, as well as correct them. To that end, we have provided a reproducible table (page 65) of some common proofreading symbols. If you choose not to distribute copies of the symbols, simply instruct students to proofread each problem and rewrite the sentences without the errors.

Where most helpful, we have also provided the number of errors in an exercise for guidance. To offer students more of a challenge, you may want to block this information ahead of time.

Please note, in certain exercises a single word might include multiple errors. In problem 100 (page 36), for example, the word *presidente* counts as two mistakes because it needs a capital letter and it is spelled incorrectly.

How to Use the CD

The companion CD includes ready-to-go Notebook™ files to use with your SMART Board™. With their large, interactive displays and opportunities for collaborative learning, SMART Boards are a smart way to teach the skills students will need to succeed in the 21st century: interpreting visual aids, marking text, synthesizing information, organizing data, evaluating Web sites, and team work. These skills are also an increasingly important part of the standards in many states. Using this dynamic tool is a perfect way to motivate even your most reluctant learner to participate. To get the most out of a whole-class activity, model one of the exercises, then have students complete one or more as a group, and follow up by distributing a reproducible version of a similar exercise.

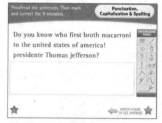

Students can use the pen tool to correct mistakes. Where appropriate, there is also a toolbar containing proofreading symbols that they can drag and drop to mark mistakes. Once satisfied that all mistakes have been corrected, students simply click on the star icon toward the bottom of the slide and drag it across the screen to place it in its matching outline to reveal the answer.

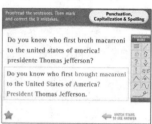

Whether you and your students are already adept at using a SMART Board or have just recently decided to give it a try, these exercises are straightforward and easy to use.

Tech Tips

The CD was created using Notebook 10 software, but you'll be able to use the activities with older versions. If you are still getting the hang of your SMART Board, be sure to look at the following overview of the main Notebook features you may use effectively for these activities.

❖ **SMART Pens** These are the black, red, green, and blue pens that came with your SMART Board. Use them to write directly on the screen in digital ink.

❖ **Creative Pens** A student favorite, this tool allows you to draw fun lines made of smiley faces, stars, rainbow stripes, and more.

❖ **Magic Pen** When students circle text with the magic pen, a spotlight focuses on the circled portion of the page. Everything else on the page goes dark temporarily. It's a dramatic way to focus attention on just one element on a page.

❖ **Eraser** Like its old-fashioned counterparts, this eraser removes unwanted writing. It will only work on text and lines created with the SMART pens, not on typed text.

❖ **On-Screen Keyboard** If your students are adding text to a small field or simply prefer typing to writing freehand, use the on-screen keyboard. You can access it by touching the keyboard icon on the front tray of your SMART Board.

❖ **Properties Tool** Use this feature to change the color or style of a SMART pen or to add color to a box.

❖ **Screen Shade** A teacher favorite, this tool allows you to cover part of a page while focusing attention on another part. Activate the shade by clicking on the Screen Shade icon on your toolbar. De-activate it by clicking it again. To gradually open a shade that covers your screen, use one of the circular buttons on the shade itself to drag the shade open.

Spelling

Name: _____

1. Cross out the 5 spelling mistakes and correct them. Then rewrite the sentence.

A camelion can moove its eyes in two

diferent direcshuns at the same tyme.

Name: _____

2. Cross out the 5 spelling mistakes and correct them. Then rewrite the sentence.

In 1899, Charles Murphy became the furst men to petal a bycicle

faster then a speeding train.

Name: _____

3. Cross out the 3 spelling mistakes and correct them. Then say the tongue twister three times fast!

Ollie's ottur aite Otto's ollive.

Name: _____

4. Unscramble the letters to spell a state name.

roNht oataDk

Name: _____

5. Cross out the 5 spelling mistakes and correct them. Then rewrite the sentences. (The person's name is spelled correctly.)

The first profesionall footboll player was Pudge Heffelfinger. In 1892, he recieved $500 too play a gayme.

Name: _____

6. Cross out the 5 spelling mistakes and correct them. Then rewrite the sentences. (The person's name is spelled correctly.)

Lou Brock was one of the gratest base steelers in baseball historey.

He stoll 938 bases in his carreer.

Name: _____

7. Cross out the 5 spelling mistakes and correct them. Then rewrite the sentences.

Most peeple have herd of a teem called the New York Mets. But that's just a knickname. Their fool name is the New York Metropolitans.

spelling

Name: _____

8. Cross out the 4 spelling mistakes and correct them. Then say the tongue twister three times fast!

Tongue Twister

Frank feested on flameing fish at the

famus Friday fish frie.

Name: _____

9. Cross out the 5 spelling mistakes and correct them. Then rewrite the sentence. (The team names are spelled correctly.)

The New York Giants and Chicago White Sox ones

plaid basball in front of the Great Piramyds in Egipt.

Name: _____

10. Cross out the 6 spelling mistakes and correct them. Then rewrite the sentences.

The gam of baskettball was invented in 1892. It was playd with a

socker ball and peech bascets.

Spelling

Name: _____

11. Cross out the 7 spelling mistakes and correct them.
Then rewrite the sentences.

Pichers are nut alowed too threw spitballs in Major Leegue Baseball.

It's ilegal!

Spelling

Name: _____

12. Cross out the 6 spelling mistakes and correct them.
Then rewrite the sentences. (The person's name is spelled correctly.)

William H. Taft startid a basball tradicion. He beecame the fist U.S.

president to throw the seremonial first pitch at a game.

Spelling

Name: _____

13. Cross out the 6 spelling mistakes and correct them.
Then say the tongue twister three times fast!

The frute fly flue threw the flute and into

the throte of the fritened fluteist.

Spelling

Name: _____

14. Cross out the 3 spelling mistakes and correct them. Then rewrite the sentences.

In 1886, Franse gave the United States a big gift: the Statute of

Liberty! She stands on an island in New York Harber.

Spelling

Name: _____

15. Cross out the 7 spelling mistakes and correct them. Then rewrite the sentences.

The werd *dinosaur* means "terrable lizerd." But not all dinosaurs were feirce. Some where peasefull plant eeters.

Spelling

Name: _____

16. Cross out the 4 spelling mistakes and correct them. Then say the tongue twister three times fast!

Fanny's flannul fabrik freqwently frayes.

Name: _____

17. Unscramble the letters to spell a state name.

n s r s a A k a

Name: _____

18. Cross out the 6 spelling mistakes and correct them.
Then rewrite the sentences.

In Sweden, their is a hottel bilt out off ice.

It melts evry spring and is rebuilt everey winter.

Name: _____

19. Cross out the 6 spelling mistakes and correct them.
Then rewrite the sentences.

The stegosaurus had a tiney brain. It was no biger then a walnut!

That's why eksperts think it was one of the dummer dinasores.

Name: _____

20. Cross out the 6 spelling mistakes and correct them.
Then rewrite the sentences.

More than 15 milion plants and animals live in the rain forrest. The

combanation of heet and moistur makes it the purfect home for them.

5-Minute Proofreading Practice

Spelling

Name: _____

Spelling

21. Cross out the 5 spelling mistakes and correct them.
Then rewrite the sentences.

Perple is a collor of royalty. It used to be verey expencive. Only

kings and queens could aford it!

Name: _____

Spelling

22. Cross out the 6 spelling mistakes and correct
them. Then rewrite the sentences.

You can create the color oranje by mixxing

yelow and read. But you can nevver find a

word to ryme with orange.

Name: _____

Spelling

23. Cross out the 7 spelling mistakes and correct them.
Then rewrite the sentences.

The Bill of Rights is part ov the U.S. Constitucion. There are ten

amenments in the Bill of Rites. The first one garanties freedom of

relijun, speach, and the press.

Name: _____

24. Unscramble the letters to spell a state name.

s i s i i p i s M s p

Name: _____

25. Cross out the 3 spelling mistakes and correct them. Then say the tongue twister three times fast!

Percy is pade plenty to painte

planes planely.

Tongue Twister

Name: _____

26. Unscramble the letters to spell a state name.

l I n o i s i l

Capitalization

Name: _____

27. Find and mark the 2 capitalization errors.

After they see a good show, many americans

clap their hands. In spain, some people

snap their fingers!

Capitalization

Name: _____

28. Find and mark the 3 capitalization errors.

Sacajawea faces right on the american Dollar coin. She was never

president, but She was an important person in American history.

Capitalization

Name: _____

29. Find and mark the 5 capitalization errors.

Walt Disney created the star of a Cartoon called *steamboat willie*.

The name of the star was mickey mouse!

Name: _____

30. Find and mark the 3 capitalization errors. Then say the tongue twister three times fast!

horrible hilda hears hairy harry holler.

Tongue Twister

Name: _____

31. Find and mark the 3 capitalization errors.

Francis scott Key wrote "The star-Spangled Banner." it's our national anthem.

Name: _____

32. Find and mark the 4 capitalization errors.

The largest planet in the Solar System is named jupiter. That's also the name of an ancient roman deity.

Name: _____

33. Find and mark the 4 capitalization errors.

boston won the first world Series ever played. The Boston

pilgrims beat the pittsburgh Pirates five games to three.

Name: _____

34. Find and mark the 5 capitalization errors.

Golf Pro tiger woods was born on december 20, 1975. His real first

name is eldrick.

Name: _____

35. Find and mark the 4 capitalization errors.

People from Wyoming are known as wyomingites.

There are about 500,000 Wyomingites in The united states.

Name: _____

36. Find and mark the 6 capitalization errors.
Then say the tongue twister three times fast!

peter potter paid a Penny for patty

peeper's Pepperoni pizza.

Name: _____

37. Find and mark the 6 capitalization errors.

The wright brothers' famous flight at kitty hawk, north carolina,

lasted less than Two minutes.

Name: _____

38. Find and mark the 5 capitalization errors.

The largest ice cream Sundae weighed

nearly 25 Tons. It was made in canada

by a company called palm dairies.

Name: _____

39. Find and mark the 6 capitalization errors.

the world's Shortest War was between england and Zanzibar. it only

lasted 38 Minutes.

Name: _____

40. Find and mark the 6 capitalization errors.

there are more english-Speaking People in china than in

the united States.

Name: _____

41. Find and mark the 5 capitalization errors.

two-Thirds of the World's Eggplant is grown in new Jersey.

Name: _____

42. Find and mark the 9 capitalization errors.

The u.s. has had three presidents named george: George washington,

George h.w. Bush, and george w. bush.

Name: _____

43. Find and mark the 5 capitalization errors.
Then say the tongue twister three times fast!

when dwight white writes, Dwight Writes Right.

Name: _____

44. Find and mark the 7 capitalization errors.

michael kearney became the World's

youngest College graduate in june 1994.

He graduated from the university of

south Alabama at the age of 10.

Name: _____

45. Find and mark the 6 capitalization errors.

Mickey mouse was banned in italy in 1938. the Government thought

mickey was unsuitable for Children.

Name: _____

46. Find and mark the 3 capitalization errors.
Then say the tongue twister three times fast!

Bob brought billy's bright Brass

bike back from boston.

Tongue Twister

Name: _____

47. Find and mark the 10 capitalization errors.

harry potter and the sorcerer's stone is one of the most popular

books of All Time. The Author's name is j.k. rowling.

Name: _____

48. Find and mark the 9 capitalization errors.

the Real name of president ulysses s. grant was hyram ulysses grant.

Name: _____

49. Find and mark the 4 capitalization errors.

england's Queen elizabeth lives in buckingHam Palace.

Name: _____

50. Find and mark the 3 capitalization errors.

a healthy Human's blood pressure

is about the same as a healthy Spider's.

Name: _____

51. Find and mark the 9 capitalization errors.

The First american president to be born in a Hospital was a former

Peanut Farmer from Plains, georgia. his name is jimmy carter.

Name: _____

52. Find and mark the 4 capitalization errors.

The largest american State is Alaska. Do You know which state

is the smallest? It's Rhode island.

Name: _____

53. Find and correct the 8 capitalization and spelling errors.
Then rewrite the sentences.

president Calvin coolidge had a pet Raccoon named rebecca.

He walkd her around the white house on a leesh.

Name: _____

54. Find and correct the 6 capitalization and spelling errors.
Then rewrite the sentence.

The First bottlle of coke was bottled in vicksburg, misisippi.

Name: _____

55. Find and correct the 4 capitalization and spelling errors.
Then say the tongue twister three times fast!

Tongue Twister

Ant edith's anteater eight aunt Edith's ants.

Name: _____

56. Find and correct the 8 capitalization and spelling errors.
Then rewrite the sentences.

the Hair Museum is in independence, Missouri. it has wierd

things made out of hare. visiters can olso get a haircut there.

Name: _____

57. Find and correct the 6 capitalization and spelling errors.
Then rewrite the sentences.

In 1998, John bain of Delaware terned his Rubber-Band

colleccion into a giant rubber-band ball. It wayed 2,000 pounds!

Name: _____

58. Find and correct the 6 capitalization and
spelling errors. Then say the tongue twister
three times fast!

carol carefuly caried cora's

colection of carotts.

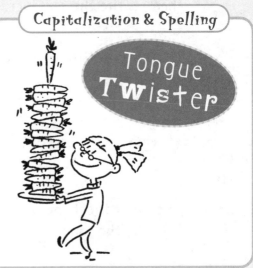

Tongue Twister

Name: _____

59. Find and correct the 7 capitalization and spelling errors.
Then rewrite the sentences.

Halve you ever wundered howe big your hart is? It's about the

some sized as yore fist.

Name: _____

60. Find and correct the 4 punctuation errors. Then rewrite the sentence.

A teenager in Miami Florida once sneezed for 155 days, in a row?

Name: _____

61. Find and correct the 4 punctuation errors. Then rewrite the sentences.

Doctor Rene Laennec invented the stethoscope! It was a rolled-up sheet of paper, The doctor put one end on a patients chest and pressed his ear to the other end;

Name: _____

62. Find and correct the 6 punctuation errors. Then rewrite the sentences.

Diane Sheer of London England, is the worlds fastest stamp licker? She licked 225 stamps; and stuck them onto envelopes. in just five minutes:

Name: _____

63. Find and correct the 2 punctuation errors. Then rewrite the sentences.

How did ancient Egyptian doctors knock out patients before surgery.

They hit them on the head with a mallet?

Name: _____

64. Find and correct the 4 punctuation errors. Then rewrite the sentences.

Many people know that: Florence

Nightingale, was a nurse Few know

that she kept a pet owl in her pocket?

Name: _____

65. Find and correct the 6 punctuation errors. Then rewrite the sentences.

Michael Jacksons *Thriller* is the best-selling album of all time; Since

it's release in 1982 more than "47 million copies" have been sold?

Punctuation

Name: _____

66. Find and correct the 6 punctuation errors. Then rewrite the sentences.

Why? should you cover your mouth when you sneeze! Particles,

from a sneeze, can travel more than: 100 miles per hour

Punctuation

Name: _____

67. Find and correct the 4 punctuation errors. Then rewrite the sentences.

In ancient China; doctors got paid if their patients stayed healthy

If a patient got sick. the doctor paid the patient!!

Punctuation

Name: _____

68. Find and correct the 7 punctuation errors. Then rewrite the sentences.

Graham crackers were named for Sylvester Graham a doctor who

lived in the 1830s' He was one of the first to recommend taking

baths eating, vegetables and exercising;

Name: _____

69. Find and correct the 5 punctuation errors. Then rewrite the sentences.

If you like peace; and quiet dont move to Tororo, Uganda. It
thunders more than 250 days a year, there?

Name: _____

70. Find and correct the 5 punctuation errors. Then rewrite the sentences.

Benjamin Franklin was a busy guy He helped create Americas first
postal system: fire department: and hospital?

Name: _____

71. Find and correct the 6 punctuation errors.
Then rewrite the sentences.

Whats that ringing! It must be the House
of Telephones, in Coffeyville; Kansas? It
has 1,000 phones

Name: _____

72. Find and correct the 7 punctuation errors. Then rewrite the sentences.

When it comes to recycling Germany wins the prize? The country

recycles, between 70 and 80 percent, of it's cardboard, and paper

Name: _____

73. Find and correct the 5 punctuation errors. Then rewrite the sentences.

North Dakota has a strange nickname. Its called the 'Flickertail State'

(A flickertail is a kind of squirrel.

Name: _____

74. Find and correct the 7 punctuation errors. Then rewrite the sentences.

Once a year Spain holds an unusual festival; The

"festival" is called La Tomatina? People throw

tomatoes at one another, for 90 minutes)

Name: _____

75. Find and correct the 4 punctuation errors. Then rewrite the sentences.

Achoo! If you sneezed, in ancient Rome: someone might have said,

Jupiter bless you"

Name: _____

76. Find and correct the 3 punctuation errors. Then rewrite the sentence.

George Washington used chalk as toothpaste before, and after,

he got false teeth,

Name: _____

77. Find and correct the 7 punctuation errors. Then rewrite the sentences.

In the 1300s' French soldiers carried

an unusual item in their first-aid kits; spiderwebs? If they got injured

theyd pack webs into the wound to stop the bleeding

Name: _____

78. Find and correct the 7 punctuation errors. Then rewrite the sentences.

Paul Revere is famous for crying "The British are coming?
The British are coming. But, did you know, that this silversmith
also worked as a dentist!

Name: _____

79. Find and correct the 4 punctuation errors. Then rewrite the sentences.

The first Super Bowl was played in 1967 in Los Angeles California
It was known as the AFC-NFC Championship game Tickets cost only
$10 each

Name: _____

80. Find and correct the 4 punctuation errors. Then rewrite the sentences.

What did the judge say, when the skunk walked into the courtroom.
"Odor in the court

Name: _____

81. Find and correct the 6 punctuation errors. Then rewrite the sentences.

It costs' about 66$ a minute to light a large baseball stadium:

Thats about $3960 per hour

Name: _____

82. Find and correct the 5 punctuation errors. Then rewrite the sentences.

US paper money isnt really printed on paper; It's printed on cloth

made of cotton and linen..

Name: _____

83. Find and correct the 3 punctuation errors. Then rewrite the sentences.

Do you collect pennies Many people do:

A mile of pennies equals $844.80?

Name: _____

84. Find and correct the 2 punctuation errors. Then rewrite the sentence.

In 1940 the average American worker earned less than $600 a year"

Name: _____

85. Find and correct the 5 punctuation errors. Then rewrite the sentences.

Its impossible to speak without using your lips and tongue If you

dont believe it try to say the alphabet this way?

Name: _____

86. Find and correct the 5 punctuation errors. Then rewrite the sentences.

If you live in Kentucky: youd better remember

to take a bath once a year; Its the law

Name: _____

87. Find and correct the 3 punctuation errors.
Then rewrite the sentences.

Your mouth produces a lot of saliva in a day

In fact—it makes enough to fill a soda can

Name: _____

88. Find and correct the 4 punctuation errors. Then rewrite the sentences.

Hungry If so! you might want to have a frog as a snack Humans eat

more than 200 million frogs each year

Name: _____

89. Find and correct the 2 punctuation errors. Then rewrite the sentence.

When horned toads are scared: they shoot blood from their eyes?

Name: _____

90. Find and correct the 6 punctuation errors. Then rewrite the sentences.

If youre not in the mood for a froggy snack: perhaps youd like a snail

In France people eat about 500 million snails a year?

Name: _____

91. Find and correct the 3 punctuation errors. Then rewrite the sentences.

Why are spicy chicken wings called Buffalo wings! They were first

made in Buffalo New York:

Name: _____

92. Find and correct the 6 punctuation errors. Then rewrite the sentences.

Whats you'r favorite pizza topping.

Green peas are popular in Brazil?

In England, corn is a favorite Australians

like to put eggs on their pizza

Name: _____

93. Find and correct the 3 punctuation errors. Then rewrite the sentences.

There is a street in Italy thats less than 1.5 feet wide

That's thinner than some people

Punctuation

Name: _____

94. Find and correct the 5 punctuation errors. Then rewrite the sentences.

Before 1922 cars didnt have gas gauges As a result; a lot of people

ran out of gas

Punctuation

Name: _____

95. Find and correct the 4 punctuation errors. Then rewrite the sentences.

Thomas Edison was a great inventor He invented the phonograph,

and improved electric lights? He also invented wax paper

Punctuation

Name: _____

96. Find and correct the 2 punctuation errors. Then rewrite the sentence.

Before Popeye started eating spinach

he got his strength from garlic

Name: _____

97. Find and correct the 4 punctuation errors. Then rewrite the sentences.

When ketchup was first made the recipe didnt include tomatoes It was made from fish broth and mushrooms

---

Name: _____

98. Find and correct the 3 punctuation errors. Then rewrite the sentences.

About 80 percent of your brain, is made of water Watermelons are 92 percent water

Name: _____

99. Find and correct the 3 punctuation errors. Then rewrite the sentences.

Coloring wasnt much fun back when Crayola started making crayons They only came in one color black!

Name: _____

100. Proofread the sentences and mark the 10 mistakes.
Then rewrite the sentences.

Do you know who first broth macarroni to the united states of

america! presidente Thomas jefferson?

Name: _____

101. Proofread the sentences and mark the 10 mistakes.
Then rewrite the sentences.

Rhode Island is the smallist stake in the

United states Its jost 48 miles, across at it's

widist point

Name: _____

102. Proofread the sentences and mark the 15 mistakes.
Then rewrite the sentences.

some mite say that louise Greenfarb, has a Magnetic Personality the

Spanway, Washington, resident has collectid more than; 29000

Refrigerater Magnets

Name: _____

Punctuation, Capitalization & Spelling

103. Proofread the sentences and mark the 16 mistakes.
Then rewrite the sentences.

Did you no that you wer born wit 350 boans in your bodey! By the time your a grown-up yule have just 206 bonz bones grow toogether as poeple grew up

---

Name: _____

Punctuation, Capitalization & Spelling

104. Proofread the sentences and mark the 15 mistakes.
Then rewrite the sentences.

manny diferent things are make from resycled items backpacks, benchs, and carpets com from recycled plastick, and bullitin bords and playground equiptment are maid from recycled rubber

---

Name: _____

Punctuation, Capitalization & Spelling

105. Proofread the sentences and mark the 6 mistakes.
Then rewrite the sentences.

The first vidoe game was invented by Noland busnell; His invencion was called Pong!

Name: _____

106. Proofread the sentences and mark the 13 mistakes.
Then rewrite the sentences.

Percy spencer invented the micowave owven by acident.. He was

testing raydar equipmint and it melted a candy bar in his pockett?

He realised microwaives could be used for cookin)

Name: _____

107. Proofread the sentences and mark the 7 mistakes.
Then rewrite the sentences.

You know youre ZiP code, but due you know what "ZIP stands for??

Its an acronym for "zone improvement plan;"

Name: _____

108. Proofread the sentences and mark the 11 mistakes. Then rewrite the sentences.

More Amercans speek english then

any other langauge: spanish is the

second-most popular language in the

U.S, folowed by french

Punctuation,
Capitalization & Spelling

Name: _____

109. Proofread the sentence and mark the 5 mistakes.
Then rewrite the sentence.

Native americans, once used wampum bedes and Beaver ferr

as money.

Punctuation,
Capitalization & Spelling

Name: _____

110. Proofread the sentences and mark the 10 mistakes.
Then rewrite the sentences.

Thomas, edison, is well-nown for his werk with electricitty; did you

know that he invented batterys!

Punctuation,
Capitalization & Spelling

Name: _____

111. Proofread the sentences and mark the 13 mistakes.
Then rewrite the sentences.

dirt makes the sky blu! Lite from the Sun is white util it reeches

Earths' atmasfere. When it hits dust and other particles in the aire:

it looks bleu

Name: _____

112. Proofread the sentences and mark the 7 mistakes.
Then rewrite the sentences.

Mars is called the "Red planet' It has a redish color becaus it's soil

has soo much iron oxide, or rust.

Name: _____

113. Proofread the sentences and mark the 14 mistakes.
Then rewrite the sentences.

will, and john Kellogg inventid cornflakes sereal; Will was an

Nutritionist. and john wus a Docter

Name: _____

114. Proofread the sentences and mark the 12 mistakes.
Then rewrite the sentences.

Nevada waz teh 36th State to joinn the Unoin? It's name meens

"Snow-covered." in spanish

Singular & Plural Nouns

Name: _____

115. Circle the correct words to complete the sentence.

Felicia bought five bouquet/bouquets of

flower/flowers from the florist.

Singular & Plural Nouns

Name: _____

116. Circle the correct word to complete the sentence.

Pegleg Pete invited thirty of his pirate/pirates buddies to a party.

Singular & Plural Nouns

Name: _____

117. Circle the correct words to complete the sentence.

Evelyn ate the entire box/boxes of strawberry/strawberries.

Name: _____

118. Circle the correct word to complete the sentence.

Six of Sherie's ship/ships sank in the sea.

Name: _____

119. Circle the correct words to complete the sentence.

Boris baked seven pie/pies for each of his

brother/brothers.

Name: _____

120. Circle the correct words to complete the sentence.

Owen owes Anwar eight dollar/dollars and one cent/cents.

Name: _____

121. Circle the correct word to complete the sentence.

Wanda walked all of Polly's poodle/poodles in the park.

Name: _____

122. Circle the correct words to complete the sentence.

Smitty smashed six of the seven tomato/tomatoes in his

collection/collections.

Name: _____

123. Circle the correct words to complete the sentence.

Sue's suitcase/suitcases was

stuffed with books/book,

ball/balls, and broccoli.

Name: _____

124. Circle the correct words to complete the sentence.

There is a can/cans of corn and a half dozen cookie/cookies

in the cabinet.

Name: _____

125. Cross out the pronoun mistake and then correct it.

Moe and Joe are brothers. Them are

identical twins.

Name: _____

126. Cross out the pronoun mistake and then correct it.

Tilly is a terrific tap-dancer. Her is going to tap in the talent show.

Name: _____

127. Cross out the pronoun mistake and then correct it.

Fred, Frank, and Frieda are in high school. We are freshmen.

Name: _____

128. Cross out the pronoun mistake and then correct it.

Just between you and I, I think Chris is cute.

Name: _____

129. Cross out the pronoun mistake and then correct it.

Bobby wants to take his toys to camp with he.

Name: _____

130. Fill in the blank with the past tense form of the verb.

Myrna (mend) _____ Milo's mittens.

Name: _____

131. Fill in the blank with the past tense form of the verb.

Wendell (walk) _____ to work with Winnifred yesterday.

Name: _____

132. Fill in the blank with the past tense form of the verb.

Penelope (pick) _____ up a pebble and (throw) _____

it into the pond.

Name: _____

133. Fill in the blank with the past tense form of the verb.

Mildred Moneybags (go) _____ outside with

her purse open. She (hear) _____ there

would be some change in the weather!

Name: _____

134. Fill in the blank with the past tense form of the verb. Then rewrite the sentence without the 3 spelling mistakes.

Lucas (take) _____ his lukky pennie evrywhere he

(go)_____ .

Name: _____

135. Fill in the blank with the past tense form of the verb.
Then rewrite the sentence without the 5 spelling mistakes.

Aunt Edna and Uncle Ernie (eat) _____ diner at a restuarant

evry uther evning.

Name: _____

136. Fill in the blank with the past tense form of
the verb. Then rewrite the sentence without
the 4 spelling mistakes.

Hank's hocky helmits (hide) _____

his horible harecut.

Name: _____

137. Use proofreading marks to insert the proper punctuation.

Are you hungry Helga asked

Name: _____

138. Use proofreading marks to insert the proper punctuation.

Youre stepping on my toe screamed Sidney

Name: _____

139. Use proofreading marks to insert the proper punctuation.

Arnie asked Annie What time is it when the

clock strikes thirteen

Punctuation & Quotation Marks

Name: _____

140. Use proofreading marks to insert the proper punctuation.

Who said It ain't over till its over Yogi Berra did

Punctuation & Quotation Marks

Name: _____

141. Use proofreading marks to insert the proper punctuation.

When Neil Armstrong set foot on the moon he said Thats one small

step for a man, one giant leap for mankind

Possessives

Name: _____

142. Circle the 3 mistakes. Then rewrite the sentence without errors.

Peter pulled the petal's off Florences flowers'.

Name: _____

143. Circle the 4 mistakes. Then rewrite the sentence without errors.

When Tinas tonsil's tickled, Tinas mother took her to Doctor Dolots office.

Name: _____

144. Circle the 3 mistakes. Then rewrite the sentence without errors.

Percys only parakeets feathers' are falling on the floor.

Name: _____

145. Circle the 2 mistakes. Then rewrite the sentence without errors.

Murrays' room is much messier than Millies room.

POSSESSIVES

Name: _____

146. Circle the 2 mistakes. Then rewrite the sentence without errors.

The Hudsons hillside house is bigger than Billy Boyds bungalow on the beach.

Name: _____

147. Circle the 3 mistakes. Then rewrite the sentences without errors.

Betsy loves to play with Bootsies bell, but Bootsie doesn't like to play with Betsys' rubber mouse. (Betsy and Bootsie are cat's.)

Name: _____

148. Circle the 3 mistakes. Then rewrite the sentence without errors.

Mrs. Pickens dancing chicken entertained the boys' and girls at Bennys barbecue.

Name: _____

149. Cross out the words that are used incorrectly. Then replace them with the correct homophones.

Frankie the florist charges fifty sense a flour.

Homophones

Name: _____

150. Cross out the words that are used incorrectly. Then replace them with the correct homophones.

Irving's insult maid Bertha cry for more than an our.

Homophones

Name: _____

151. Cross out the word that is used incorrectly. Then replace it with the correct homophone.

Milton threw his shoo at the flies.

Homophones

Name: _____

152. Cross out the words that are used incorrectly. Then replace them with the correct homophones.

Ernie eight won beet and two tomatoes for supper.

Name: _____

153. Cross out the words that are used incorrectly. Then replace them with the correct homophones.

Gary received ate letters in the male.

Name: _____

154. Cross out the words that are used incorrectly. Then replace them with the correct homophones.

The champion swimmer one

a gold metal!

Name: _____

155. Cross out the words that are used incorrectly. Then replace them with the correct homophones.

When a dear ran in front of the car, Sammy slammed on the breaks.

Name: _____

156. Cross out the words that are used incorrectly. Then replace them with the correct homophones.

When Lola stubbed her tow, it was soar for daze.

Verb Use

Name: _____

157. Cross out the verb that is used incorrectly. Then rewrite the sentence.

When Irving called Bertha a big baby, he really meaned it.

Verb Use

Name: _____

158. Cross out the verb that is used incorrectly. Then rewrite the sentence.

Bertha bursted into tears when Irving insulted her.

Verb Use

Name: _____

159. Cross out the verbs that are used incorrectly. Then rewrite the sentences.

The batter swing at the ball, but he miss it. The umpire say, "Strike three!"

Subject/Verb Agreement

Verb Use

Name: _____

160. Cross out the verbs that are used incorrectly. Then rewrite the sentences.

Mindy is happy she bring mittens on the

camping trip. Without them, her fingers might have freezed.

Verb Use

Name: _____

161. Cross out the verbs that are used incorrectly. Then rewrite the sentences.

Stanley was glad he go to the class reunion.

He hadn't saw some of his classmates in years.

Subject/Verb Agreement

Name: _____

162. Rewrite the sentence so that the subject and verb agree.

"Eighty divided by ten equal eight," stated Stevie.

Name: _____

163. Rewrite the sentence so that the subject and verb agree.

Some of the children is too small to ride the roller coaster.

Name: _____

164. Rewrite the sentence so that the subject and verb agree.

Many of the runners has won a marathon.

Name: _____

165. Rewrite the sentences so that the subjects and verbs agree.

People in Paramus is very friendly. The ones that lives on Montana Street is the friendliest of all.

Name: _____

166. Rewrite the sentences so that the subjects and verbs agree.

Both the sets and costumes was wonderful in the play. The actors wasn't.

Name: _____

167. Rewrite the sentence so that the subject and the verb agree.

"My rubber nose are missing!" cried the melancholy clown.

Name: _____

168. Rewrite the sentence so that the subject and the verb agree.

Bruno get sick when he rides a roller coaster, but Bruce don't.

Name: _____

169. Proofread for double negatives. Correct the sentence by changing one of the negative words.

My little brother can't go nowhere without asking

permission first.

Name: _____

170. Proofread for double negatives. Correct the sentence by changing one of the negative words.

Suzy couldn't finish no more dinner

because she was full.

Name: _____

171. Proofread for double negatives. Correct the sentence by changing one of the negative words.

Donny didn't feel nothing after the

magician waved his wand.

Double Negatives

Name: _____

172. Proofread for double negatives. Correct the sentence by changing one of the negative words.

You can't teach an old dog nothing new.

Double Negatives

Name: _____

173. Proofread for double negatives. Correct the sentence by changing one of the negative words.

Don't tell nobody Cindy's secret!

Adverbs

Name: _____

174. Cross out the adverb mistake and then correct it.

Queen Lucille likes to speak quiet.

Name: _____

175. Cross out the adverb mistake and then correct it.

The batter watched the pitch very close.

Name: _____

176. Cross out the adverb mistake and then correct it.

The pitcher threw the baseball careful.

Name: _____

177. Cross out the adverb mistake and then correct it.

The pilot landed the plane
safe in the snowstorm.

Adverbs

Name: _____

178. Cross out the adverb mistake and then correct it.

Eat slow, or you may get a stomachache.

Adverbs

Name: _____

179. Cross out the adverb mistake and then correct it.

In a spelling bee, it's important to speak clear.

Adverbs

Name: _____

180. Cross out the adverb mistake and then correct it.

Lulu walks quick when she's late for school.

Answers

1. A chameleon can move its eyes in two different directions at the same time.

2. In 1899, Charles Murphy became the first man to pedal a bicycle faster than a speeding train.

3. Ollie's otter ate Otto's olive.

4. North Dakota

5. The first professional football player was Pudge Heffelfinger. In 1892, he received $500 to play a game.

6. Lou Brock was one of the greatest base stealers in baseball history. He stole 938 bases in his career.

7. Most people have heard of a team called the New York Mets. But that's just a nickname. Their full name is the New York Metropolitans.

8. Frank feasted on flaming fish at the famous Friday fish fry.

9. The New York Giants and Chicago White Sox once played baseball in front of the Great Pyramids in Egypt.

10. The game of basketball was invented in 1892. It was played with a soccer ball and peach baskets.

11. Pitchers are not allowed to throw spitballs in Major League Baseball. It's illegal!

12. William H. Taft started a baseball tradition. He became the first U.S. president to throw the ceremonial first pitch at a game.

13. The fruit fly flew through the flute and into the throat of the frightened flutist.

14. In 1886, France gave the United States a big gift: the Statue of Liberty! She stands on an island in New York Harbor.

15. The word *dinosaur* means "terrible lizard." But not all dinosaurs were fierce. Some were peaceful plant eaters.

16. Fanny's flannel fabric frequently frays.

17. Arkansas

18. In Sweden, there is a hotel built out of ice. It melts every spring and is rebuilt every winter.

19. The stegosaurus had a tiny brain. It was no bigger than a walnut! That's why experts think it was one of the dumber dinosaurs.

20. More than 15 million plants and animals live in the rain forest. The combination of heat and moisture makes it the perfect home for them.

21. Purple is a color of royalty. It used to be very expensive. Only kings and queens could afford it!

22. You can create the color orange by mixing yellow and red. But you can never find a word to rhyme with orange.

23. The Bill of Rights is part of the U.S. Constitution. There are ten amendments in the Bill of Rights. The first one guarantees freedom of religion, speech, and the press.

24. Mississippi

25. Percy is paid plenty to paint planes plainly.

26. Illinois

27. After they see a good show, many americans clap their hands. In spain, some people snap their fingers!

28. Sacajawea faces right on the american Dollar coin. She was never president, but She was an important person in American history.

29. Walt Disney created the star of a Cartoon called *steamboat willie*. The name of the star was mickey mouse!

30. horrible hilda hears hairy harry holler.

31. Francis scott Key wrote "The star-Spangled Banner." it's our national anthem.

32. The largest planet in the Solar System is named jupiter. That's also the name of an ancient roman deity.

33. boston won the first world Series ever played. The Boston pilgrims beat the pittsburgh Pirates five games to three.

34. Golf Pro tiger woods was born on december 20, 1975. His real first name is eldrick.

35. People from Wyoming are known as wyomingites. There are about 500,000 Wyomingites in The united states.

36. peter potter paid a Penny for patty peeper's Pepperoni pizza.

37. The wright brothers' famous flight at kitty hawk, north carolina, lasted less than Two minutes.

38. The largest ice cream Sundae weighed nearly 25 Tons. It was made in canada by a company called palm dairies.

39. the world's Shortest War was between england and Zanzibar. it only lasted 38 Minutes.

40. there are more english-Speaking People in china than in the united States.

41. two-Thirds of the World's Eggplant is grown in new Jersey.

42. The u.s. has had three presidents named george: George washington, George h.w. Bush, and george w. bush.

43. when dwight white writes, Dwight Writes Right.

44. michael kearney became the World's youngest College graduate in june 1994. He graduated from the university of south Alabama at the age of 10.

45. Mickey mouse was banned in italy in 1938. the Government thought mickey was unsuitable for Children.

46. Bob brought billy's bright Brass bike back from boston.

47. *harry potter and the sorcerer's stone* is one of the most popular books of All Time. The Author's name is j.k. rowling.

48. the Real name of president ulysses s. grant was hyram ulysses grant.

49. england's Queen elizabeth lives in buckingHam Palace.

50. a healthy Human's blood pressure is about the same as a healthy Spider's.

51. The First american president to be born in a Hospital was a former Peanut Farmer from Plains, georgia. his name is jimmy carter.

52. The largest american State is Alaska. Do You know which state is the smallest? It's Rhode island.

53. President Calvin Coolidge had a pet raccoon named Rebecca. He walked her around the White House on a leash.

54. The first bottle of Coke was bottled in Vicksburg, Mississippi.

55. Aunt Edith's anteater ate Aunt Edith's ants.

56. The Hair Museum is in Independence, Missouri. It has weird things made out of hair. Visitors can also get a haircut there.

57. In 1998, John Bain of Delaware turned his rubber-band collection into a giant rubber-band ball. It weighed 2,000 pounds!

58. Carol carefully carried Cora's collection of carrots

59. Have you ever wondered how big your heart is? It's about the same size as your fist.

60. A teenager in Miami, Florida, once sneezed for 155 days in a row.

61. Doctor Rene Laennec invented the stethoscope. It was a rolled-up sheet of paper. The doctor put one end on a patient's chest and pressed his ear to the other end.

62. Diane Sheer of London, England, is the world's fastest stamp licker. She licked 225 stamps and stuck them onto envelopes in just five minutes.

63. How did ancient Egyptian doctors knock out patients before surgery? They hit them on the head with a mallet!

64. Many people know that Florence Nightingale was a nurse. Few know that she kept a pet owl in her pocket.

65. Michael Jackson's *Thriller* is the best-selling album of all time. Since its release in 1982 more than 47 million copies have been sold.

66. Why should you cover your mouth when you sneeze? Particles from a sneeze can travel more than 100 miles per hour!

67. In ancient China, doctors got paid if their patients stayed healthy. If a patient got sick, the doctor paid the patient!

68. Graham crackers were named for Sylvester Graham, a doctor who lived in the 1830's. He was one of the first to recommend taking baths, eating vegetables, and exercising.

69. If you like peace and quiet, don't move to Tororo, Uganda. It thunders more than 250 days a year there!

70. Benjamin Franklin was a busy guy. He helped create America's first postal system, fire department, and hospital.

71. What's that ringing? It must be the House of Telephones in Coffeyville, Kansas. It has 1,000 phones.

72. When it comes to recycling, Germany wins the prize. The country recycles between 70 and 80 percent of its cardboard and paper.

73. North Dakota has a strange nickname. It's called the "Flickertail State." (A flickertail is a kind of squirrel.)

74. Once a year, Spain holds an unusual festival. The festival is called La Tomatina. People throw tomatoes at one another for 90 minutes.

75. Achoo! If you sneezed in ancient Rome, someone might have said, "Jupiter bless you."

76. George Washington used chalk as toothpaste before and after he got false teeth.

77. In the 1300's, French soldiers carried an unusual item in their first-aid kits: spiderwebs. If they got injured, they'd pack webs into the wound to stop the bleeding.

78. Paul Revere is famous for crying, "The British are coming! The British are coming!" But did you know that this silversmith also worked as a dentist?

79. The first Super Bowl was played in 1967 in Los Angeles, California. It was known as the AFC-NFC Championship game. Tickets cost only $10 each.

80. What did the judge say when the skunk walked into the courtroom? "Odor in the court!"

81. It costs about $66 a minute to light a large baseball stadium. That's about $3,960 per hour.

82. U.S. paper money isn't really printed on paper. It's printed on cloth made of cotton and linen.

83. Do you collect pennies? Many people do. A mile of pennies equals $844.80.

84. In 1940, the average American worker earned less than $600 a year.

85. It's impossible to speak without using your lips and tongue. If you don't believe it, try to say the alphabet this way.

86. If you live in Kentucky, you'd better remember to take a bath once a year. It's the law.

87. Your mouth produces a lot of saliva in a day. In fact, it makes enough to fill a soda can.

88. Hungry? If so, you might want to have a frog as a snack. Humans eat more than 200 million frogs each year.

89. When horned toads are scared, they shoot blood from their eyes.

90. If you're not in the mood for a froggy snack, perhaps you'd like a snail. In France, people eat about 500 million snails a year!

91. Why are spicy chicken wings called Buffalo wings? They were first made in Buffalo, New York.

92. What's your favorite pizza topping? Green peas are popular in Brazil. In England, corn is a favorite. Australians like to put eggs on their pizza.

93. There is a street in Italy that's less than 1.5 feet wide. That's thinner than some people!

94. Before 1922, cars didn't have gas gauges. As a result, a lot of people ran out of gas.

95. Thomas Edison was a great inventor. He invented the phonograph and improved electric lights. He also invented wax paper.

96. Before Popeye started eating spinach, he got his strength from garlic.

97. When ketchup was first made, the recipe didn't include tomatoes. It was made from fish broth and mushrooms.

98. About 80 percent of your brain is made of water. Watermelons are 92 percent water.

99. Coloring wasn't much fun back when Crayola started making crayons. They only came in one color: black!

100. Do you know who first brought macaroni to the United States of America? President Thomas Jefferson.

101. Rhode Island is the smallest state in the United States. It's just 48 miles across at its widest point.

102. Some might say that Louise Greenfarb has a magnetic personality. The Spanway, Washington, resident has collected more than 29,000 refrigerator magnets.

103. Did you know that you were born with 350 bones in your body? By the time you're a grown-up, you'll have just 206 bones. Bones grow together as people grow up.

104. Many different things are made from recycled items. Backpacks, benches, and carpets come from recycled plastic, and bulletin boards and playground equipment are made from recycled rubber.

105. The first video game was invented by Noland Busnell. His invention was called Pong.

106. Percy Spencer invented the microwave oven by accident. He was testing radar equipment and it melted a candy bar in his pocket. He realized microwaves could be used for cooking!

107. You know your ZIP code, but do you know what "ZIP" stands for? It's an acronym for "zone improvement plan."

108. More Americans speak English than any other language. Spanish is the second-most popular language in the U.S., followed by French.

109. Native Americans once used wampum beads and beaver fur as money.

110. Thomas Edison is well-known for his work with electricity. Did you know that he invented batteries?

111. Dirt makes the sky blue. Light from the sun is white until it reaches Earth's atmosphere. When it hits dust and other particles in the air, it looks blue.

112. Mars is called the "Red Planet." It has a reddish color because its soil has so much iron oxide, or rust.

113. Will and John Kellogg invented cornflakes cereal. Will was a nutritionist and John was a doctor.

114. Nevada was the 36th state to join the Union. Its name means "snow-covered" in Spanish.

115. bouquets; flowers

116. pirate

117. box; strawberries

118. ships

119. pies; brothers

120. dollars; cent

121. poodles

122. tomatoes; collection

123. suitcase; books; balls

124. can; cookies

125. Them; They

126. Her; She

127. We; They

128. (you and) I; me

129. he; him

130. mended

131. walked

132. picked; threw

133. went; heard

134. Lucas took his lucky penny everywhere he went.

135. Aunt Edna and Uncle Ernie ate dinner at a restaurant every other evening.

136. Hank's hockey helmet hid his horrible haircut.

137. "Are you hungry?" Helga asked.

138. "You're stepping on my toe!" screamed Sidney.

139. Arnie asked Annie, "What time is it when the clock strikes thirteen?"

140. Who said, "It ain't over till it's over"? Yogi Berra did.

141. When Neil Armstrong set foot on the moon he said, "That's one small step for a man, one giant leap for mankind."

142. Peter pulled the petals off Florence's flowers.

143. When Tina's tonsils tickled, Tina's mother took her to Doctor Dolot's office.

144. Percy's only parakeet's feathers are falling on the floor.

145. Murray's room is much messier than Millie's room.

146. The Hudsons' hillside house is bigger than Billy Boyd's bungalow on the beach.

147. Betsy loves to play with Bootsie's bell, but Bootsie won't play with Betsy's rubber mouse. (Betsy and Bootsie are cats.)

148. Mrs. Picken's dancing chicken entertained the boys and girls at Benny's barbecue.

149. sense, cents; flour, flower

150. maid, made; our, hour

151. shoo, shoe

152. eight, ate; won, one

153. ate, eight; male, mail

154. one, won; metal, medal

155. dear, deer; breaks, brakes

156. tow, toe; soar, sore; daze, days

157. When Irving called Bertha a big baby, he really meant it.

158. Bertha burst into tears when Irving insulted her.

159. The batter swung at the ball, but he missed it. The umpire said, "Strike three!"

160. Mindy is happy she brought mittens on the camping trip. Without them, her fingers might have frozen.

161. Stanley was glad he went to the class reunion. He hadn't seen some of his classmates in years.

162. "Eighty divided by ten equals eight," stated Stevie.

163. Some of the children are too small to ride the roller coaster.

164. Many of the runners have won a marathon.

165. People in Paramus are very friendly. The ones that live on Montana Street are the friendliest of all.

166. Both the sets and costumes were wonderful in the play. The actors weren't.

167. "My rubber nose is missing!" cried the melancholy clown.

168. Bruno gets sick when he rides a roller coaster, but Bruce doesn't.

169. My little brother can't go anywhere without asking permission first.

170. Suzy couldn't finish any more dinner because she was full.

171. Donny didn't feel anything after the magician waved his wand.

172. You can't teach an old dog anything new.

173. Don't tell anybody Cindy's secret!

174. Queen Lucille likes to speak quietly.

175. The batter watched the pitch very closely.

176. The pitcher threw the baseball carefully.

177. The pilot landed the plane safely in the snowstorm.

178. Eat slowly, or you may get a stomachache.

179. In a spelling bee, it's important to speak clearly.

180. Lulu walks quickly when she's late for school.